We Are The Wackadoodles

IT'S NICE TO BE KIND

T.A. DUGGAN

Quantum
Discovery
A LITERARY AGENC

ISBN
978−1−960197−99−3 (Paperback)
978−1−961601−00−0 (eBook)
978−1−960197−98−6 (Hardcover)

WE ARE THE WACKADOODLE'S

IT'S NICE TO BE KIND

This book belongs to:

_____

Mr. Wackadoodle and I want to teach our children the importance of being KIND and to have good MANNERS.

Although we expect our children to be nice in all situations, we know there may be times that may be difficult for them, due to challenging situations from their peers. We still want them to think through this challenging situation and encourage them to do what is best.

We are planning a family outing today and we are going to the park to play sports and have a picnic. We are all excited to spend the day together and welcome our cousin to our outing. Her name is Evelyn and we all call her June Bug because her middle name is June and she's as cute as a bug. June Bug lives on the next block with her mom and dad, Holly and Michael. We hope to see them often, as they are very special to us!!

We like to celebrate family as often as possible so that we always know how special we are to each other.

Once we arrive to the park, we all help unload the car and set up for SPORTS, FUN, AND FOOD!!!

The boys assemble the volleyball net, the bean bag toss game and the softball field. We will start by tossing around the football before we have a spirited game with the whole family.

The girls help me get the food ready by the grill and picnic tables. We set up like we do at home, which is a buffet line, which helps everyone get their food quickly to eat.

We will play some games before we eat, so we all have big appetites and will enjoy our meal together.

We start by tossing the football around and play a friendly game with the whole family. We pick teams and begin the game. We always have fun because we tease each other, as we are not all good at sports, but we like to learn and keep trying.

L.J. Grant and Jerry have an amazing ability to throw the football and sometimes it goes into the bushes. Sure enough, Jerry threw the ball and it went way over Chandy's head!! Since Chandy didn't catch the ball, he went to get it from the bushes.

When he got to the bushes, he saw three boys with the ball and asked them nicely to give it back to him. The boys told Chandy that since they found the ball, it now belongs to them. When Chandy didn't come back right away, L.J. Grant, Dorian and Jerry went to find him. When they arrived, they saw the three boys and heard Chandy ask for the ball again, but they refused to return the ball and were laughing about it.

What should L.J. Grant, Dorian, Chandy and Jerry do? They know to start by being nice and polite, but this time it did not work. They didn't know what to do next because the three boys were being mean.

Mr. Wackadoodle and I went to see what was taking the boys so long to get the football and when we arrived, those three boys were mean to us as well.

I decided to ask the boys why they would not give us back the football when they found it, and they told us that their older brothers told them that if you find something, you can keep it!

10

IS THIS TRUE?????
NO, THIS IS NOT TRUE!!!!
Why isn't this true?

When we find something that does not belong to us, we can try to find the person who lost it or turn it into a lost and found, but it is not rightfully ours to keep because we did not pay for it and the person who lost it, is probably sad and wants it back.

12

I realized that Mr. Wackadoodle and I were not going to get our football back, so I decided to ask the three boys to join us for some food and fun. The three of them looked at me very strangely and laughed at us, but they realized that I was serious with my invitation for them to join us. I asked them their names and they told us their names were Kyle, Denya, and Norton.

14

Kyle, Denya and Norton did give us back our football after they saw how important it was to us and how our family rallied together and invited them to join us for some more fun.

Since they were the same ages as L.J. Grant, Dorian and Jerry, they sat next to each other on the picnic blanket. Kyle, Denya and Norton enjoyed the food and even went back for a second helping, as there was plenty for everyone to have 2 or 3 helpings.

Mr. Wackadoodle and I welcomed the boys to join us anytime, providing they are KIND and bring their MANNERS.

We proceeded to play other games in the park and enjoyed the weather, since it was a super sunny day. We played the bean bag toss, which is so much fun, except I can never get that bag into any of those silly holes.

Throwing the Frisbee seems to be easier because nobody in our family is very good at this, so we are all equally bad at this sport and we have a good time laughing at each other. The girls all decided to go to the swings and do their own thing! After they finished on the swings, they returned to the volleyball area and we all played volleyball and have a great time!

Spending time in the park is quality time we share with our entire family. We want Kyle, Denton, and Norton to know that we are happy to include them in our family functions and they each were very happy to know that they have this opportunity to have more friends.

It is not always easy to be nice to people who are not being nice to us, but we need to remember, that being mean is not right either. This means that when we have conflict with others, it is always best to be nice first. If being nice does not work, sometimes we need to walk away.

When we arrive home, we all sit around the dining table to discuss our day. We want to focus on the boys who took the football and make sure the kids know why Mr. Wackadoodle and I handled the matter the way we did. Once the kids had an understanding, we finished our day with a group hug and we got ready to finish homework and took showers and baths and got ready for bed.

22

WHAT DID WE LEARN FROM THIS STORY???

It's Nice to be Kind means it makes us feel good to be kind because being mean is hurtful and does not end well. If everyone could be nice and have good manners, we may have a happier world around us. Being mean doesn't get us anywhere in life and it just brings on more bad feelings. Since Mr. Wackadoodle and I tell our children every day when they leave for school to have a wonderful day and be kind, they know how much we love and care for them.

Let's look at the scenarios that we have below and try to decide how you would handle the situation:

Mason approaches you and tells you to give him your lunch bag or he will fight you for it. Is Mason being mean, or just kidding around with you??

Mason is being mean and wants your lunch bag. Do you give it to him? Not at first. What do you do first? You first ask him why he doesn't have his own lunch and you will not give him your lunch, but you are happy to share it with him. If this doesn't work and he is still being mean and wants the whole lunch, then you tell your teacher that Mason doesn't have a lunch and that you want to give him your lunch. This way, the teacher is aware of his behavior, but you did not get him into trouble. We later found that Mason doesn't have a family that has enough money to pay for Mason to have a lunch, and that is why we cannot be mean to him.

Let's look at another situation: if you are on the playground and Terrance approaches you while laughing and tells you that your cap does not match your shirt and shorts. Is Terrance being mean or is he just teasing you? He is just teasing you because he was having fun with you and wanted to make a joke. You have known Terrance for 4 years and know that he likes to joke around with people, which makes us laugh too!

You should really know the difference between the word mean and the word teasing. There is a big difference. If you ever feel that someone is being mean and will not stop being mean, please find an adult and tell them because we don't want anyone to get hurt.

26

We will see mean people throughout are childhood and even as an adult, and how you respond can make all the difference in the outcome.

Mom and dad will help you, and always remember that

IT IS NEVER WRONG TO BE KIND!!!!!!!

Please join us in our next adventure, it's going to be lots and lots of fun!!!!!

LOVE,
THE WACKADODLE'S

www.ingramcontent.com/pod-product-compliance
Lightning Source LLC
LaVergne TN
LVHW070121100526
838202LV00011B/326